CHAPTER

7 Counting Money

Find some ways to spend $1.00.

SCHOOL HOME CONNECTION

Dear Family,

Today we started Chapter 7. We will count with coins to $1.00, using combinations of pennies, nickels, dimes, quarters, and half-dollars. Here are the math vocabulary words and an activity for us to do together at home.

Love,

____

My Math Words

half-dollar
one dollar

Vocabulary

half-dollar A coin worth 50¢

one dollar A bill worth 100¢

Visit *The Learning Site* for additional ideas and activities. www.harcourtschool.com

ACTIVITY

Ask your child to choose one grocery item that costs $1.00 or less. Have him or her use pennies, nickels, dimes, and quarters to show what coins could be used to buy the item.

Books to Share

To read about money with your child, look for these books in your local library.

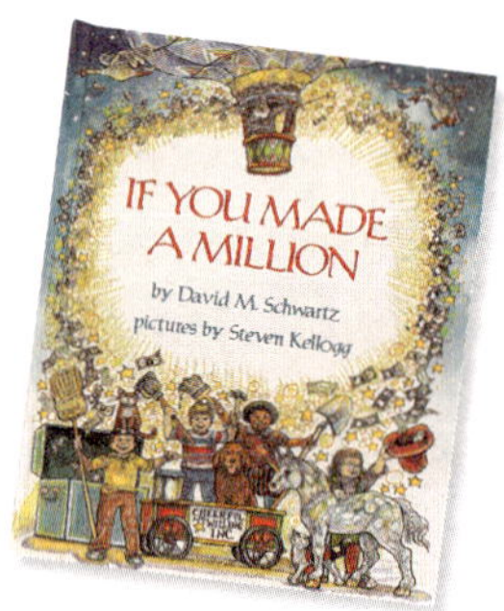

If You Made a Million,
by David M. Schwartz,
William Morrow, 1994.

Alexander Who Used to Be Rich Last Sunday,
by Judith Viorst,
Aladdin, 1980.

Lilly's Purple Plastic Purse,
by Kevin Henkes,
William Morrow, 1998.

Name ______________________________

Pennies, Nickels, and Dimes

Count by tens. **Count by fives.** **Count by ones.**

10¢ 20¢ 30¢ 35¢ 40¢ 45¢ 46¢ 47¢

1 dime = 10¢ 1 nickel = 5¢ 1 penny = 1¢

47¢ is the total amount.

Count on to find the total amount.

1

10 ¢, 20 ¢, 25 ¢, 30 ¢, 35 ¢, 36 ¢ [36] ¢

2

____ ¢, ____ ¢, ____ ¢, ____ ¢, ____ ¢, ____ ¢ [ ] ¢

3

____ ¢, ____ ¢, ____ ¢, ____ ¢, ____ ¢, ____ ¢ [ ] ¢

4

____ ¢, ____ ¢, ____ ¢, ____ ¢, ____ ¢, ____ ¢ [ ] ¢

Talk About It ■ **Reasoning**

Why does skip-counting help you count coins more quickly?

Practice

Count on to find the total amount.

1 

10 ¢, 20 ¢, 30 ¢, 40 ¢, 45 ¢, 50 ¢ [50] ¢

2 

_____ ¢, _____ ¢, _____ ¢, _____ ¢, _____ ¢, _____ ¢ [ ] ¢

3 

_____ ¢, _____ ¢, _____ ¢, _____ ¢, _____ ¢ _____ ¢ [ ] ¢

4 

_____ ¢, _____ ¢, _____ ¢, _____ ¢, _____ ¢, _____ ¢ [ ] ¢

Problem Solving ■ Reasoning

5 I have 3 coins in my purse. I have 25¢. Picture the coins in your mind. Which coins do I have?

HOME ACTIVITY • Have your child practice counting groups of mixed coins to 50¢.

Name ____________________

Quarters and Half-Dollars

1 quarter = 25¢

1 half-dollar = 50¢

Count on to find the total amount.

Start at 25. Count on 10. Count on 5. Count on 1.

1

25 ¢, 35 ¢, 40 ¢, 41 ¢ [41] ¢

2

_____ ¢, _____ ¢, _____ ¢, _____ ¢, _____ ¢, _____ ¢ [ ] ¢

3

_____ ¢, _____ ¢, _____ ¢, _____ ¢, _____ ¢, _____ ¢ [ ] ¢

Talk About It ▪ Reasoning

What groups of nickels, dimes, and quarters have the same value as 1 half-dollar?

Practice

Count on to find the total amount.

1 

50¢, 75¢, 80¢, 85¢, 90¢, 91¢ [91]¢

2 

____¢, ____¢, ____¢, ____¢, ____¢, ____¢ [ ]¢

3 

____¢, ____¢, ____¢, ____¢, ____¢, ____¢ [ ]¢

4 

____¢, ____¢, ____¢, ____¢, ____¢, ____¢ [ ]¢

Algebra

5 An apple costs 35¢. Mark does not have enough money to buy one. He needs 10¢ more. How much money does he have? ____¢

HOME ACTIVITY • **Have your child practice counting groups of mixed coins to 99¢.**

Name ______________________

Count Collections

Draw and label the coins in order from greatest to least value. Write the total amount.

1

_______ ¢

2

_______ ¢

3

_______ ¢

Talk About It ▪ Reasoning

If there were one more dime in each group on this page, how would your answers change?

Practice

Draw and label the coins in order from greatest to least value. Write the total amount.

1

55 ¢

2

_____ ¢

3

_____ ¢

4

_____ ¢

Mixed Review

Write >, <, or = in the circle.

5 7¢ ◯ 70¢ **6** 25¢ ◯ 25¢ **7** 15¢ ◯ 13¢

HOME ACTIVITY • Set out a group of coins with a total of up to 99¢. Have your child order them from greatest to least value and tell the total amount.

Name ____________________

1 Dollar

You can show $1.00 with 100 pennies.

decimal point
↓
dollar sign → $1.00

one dollar

100¢

Use coins. Show $1.00 with the coins named.
Draw and label the coins. Write the amount.

1 half-dollars

$1.00

2 quarters

______

3 dimes

______

4 nickels

______

Talk About It ■ **Reasoning**

How many ways can you show $1.00 if all the coins are the same each time?

Practice

Use coins. Show other ways to make $1.00.
Write how many of each coin.

1	1	1	2	1	0
2					
3					
4					
5					
6					
7					

Problem Solving ▪ Reasoning

Use coins.
Solve.

8 You have 11 coins. Together the coins equal $1.00. What coins could you have?

HOME ACTIVITY • Have your child use coins to show $1.00 in as many ways as possible.

Name ______________________________

UNDERSTAND › PLAN › SOLVE › CHECK

Problem Solving
Draw a Picture

Food	Price
grapes	52¢
banana	35¢
apple	68¢
orange	45¢

Use the table to solve the problems.
Choose coins to buy each food.
Draw the coins you used.

1. an orange

2. grapes

3. an apple

4. a banana

Practice

Food	Price
roll	39¢
bagel	65¢
muffin	79¢
toast	37¢

Use the table to solve the problems.
Choose coins to buy each food.
Draw the coins you used.

1. a muffin

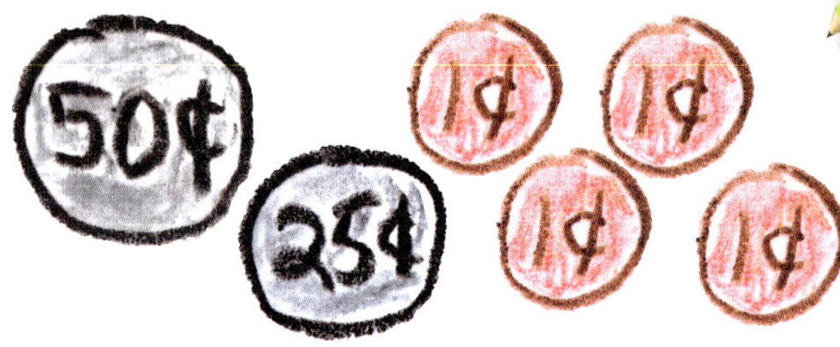

2. toast

3. a roll

4. a bagel

Math Journal

Write About It

Write about something you can buy.
Draw and label the coins you would use to buy it.

HOME ACTIVITY • Set out an item that costs up to 99¢. Have your child show you the coins that could be used to buy it.

Name ______________________________

Review/Test
Chapter 7

CHECK ■ Concepts and Skills

Count on to find the total amount.

1

_____¢, _____¢, _____¢, _____¢, _____¢, _____¢ [ ] ¢

Draw and label the coins in order from greatest to least value. Write the total amount.

2

_____

Use coins. Show $1.00 with the coins named. Draw and label the coins. Write the amount.

3 dimes

_____

CHECK ■ Problem Solving

Use coins to show the price. Draw the coins you used.

4 John buys honey. What coins can he use?

Name ______________________________

Standardized Test Prep
Chapters 1–7

Choose the best answer for questions 1–3.

1 What is the total amount?

30¢	47¢	50¢	52¢
○	○	○	○

2 David has these coins. Which toy can he buy?

○	○	○	○

3 Which numbers have the same sum as 7 + 2?

0 + 7	1 + 7	2 + 7	3 + 4
○	○	○	○

Show What You Know

4 Write a price that is less than $1.00. Draw coins to show the price. Put the coins in order from greatest to least value.

CHAPTER

8 Using Money

What are some different coins you could use to buy the doll? Which way uses the fewest coins?

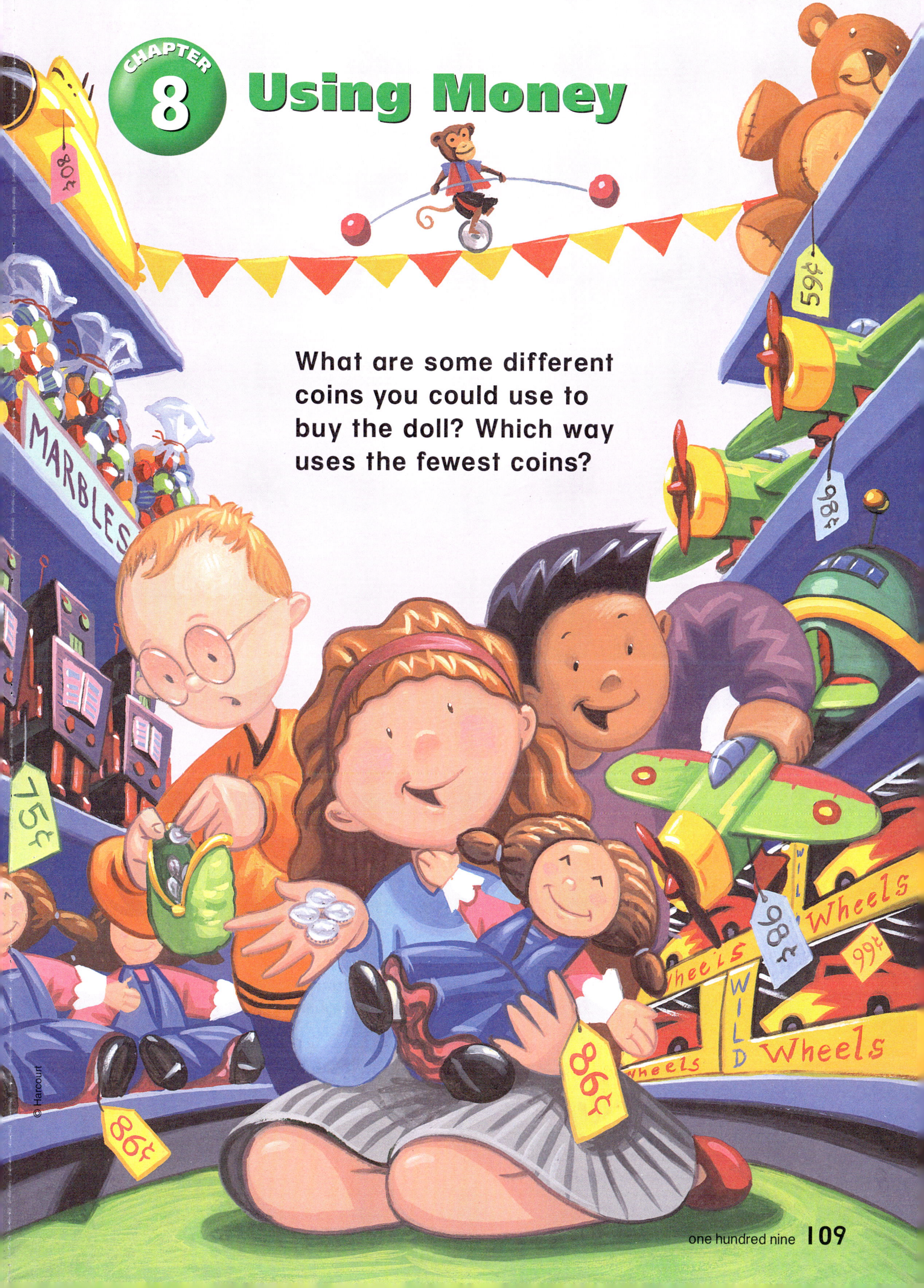

SCHOOL HOME CONNECTION

Dear Family,

Today we started Chapter 8. We will learn to show amounts of money. We will also learn to compare prices and to make change. Here is the math vocabulary and an activity for us to do together at home

Love,

____

My Math Word

change

Vocabulary

change The difference between the price of an item and the amount you give the clerk. The clerk will give back change.

39¢, 40¢

2¢ **change**

Visit *The Learning Site* for additional ideas and activities. www.harcourtschool.com

ACTIVITY

As you and your child shop, let him or her pick out an item that costs $1.00 or less. Give your child more than enough coins to buy the item. Ask him or her to choose the coins needed to pay for the item.

Books to Share

To read more stories about money with your child, look for these books in your local library.

Arthur's Funny Money,
by Lillian Hoban,
HarperCollins, 1981.

The Donkey and the Rock,
by Demi,
Henry Holt, 1999.

Market Day,
by Eve Bunting,
HarperCollins, 1999.

Name ______________________________

Make the Same Amounts

Hands On

Use coins.
Show the amount of money in two ways.
Draw and label each coin.

1 79¢		
2 96¢		
3 67¢		

Talk About It ■ **Reasoning**

What is the largest amount you can show with 2 coins? What is the smallest?

Practice

Use coins. Show the amount of money in two ways.
Draw and label each coin.

1 58¢

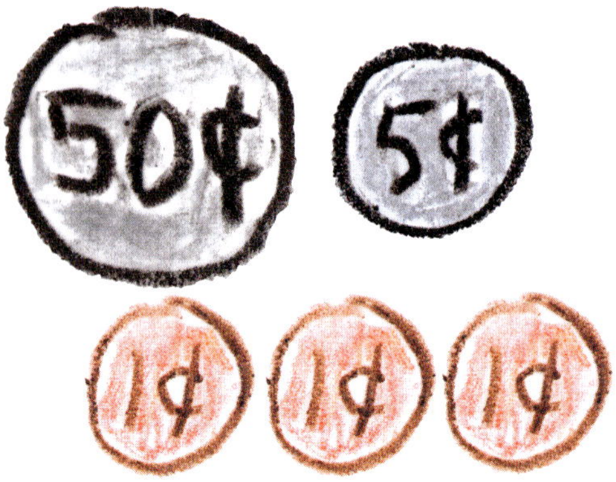

2 83¢

3 99¢

Mixed Review

Continue the pattern.

4 30¢, 40¢, 50¢, ______, ______, ______, ______

HOME ACTIVITY • Set out a group of pennies, nickels, dimes, and quarters. Work with your child to show 50¢ in as many different ways as possible.

Name ______________________________

Same Amounts Using Fewest Coins

Hands On Algebra

Write the amount. Then show the same amount with the fewest coins. Draw and label each coin.

1

75¢

2

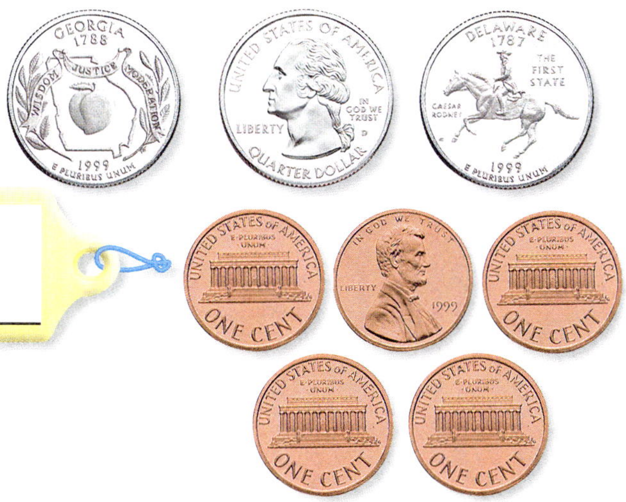

3

Talk About It ■ **Reasoning**

How can you show 99¢ with the fewest coins?

Practice

Write the amount. Then show the same amount with the fewest coins. Draw and label each coin.

1

90¢

2

3

HOME ACTIVITY • **Set out a group of coins with a total of 99¢ or less. Have your child show the same amount with the fewest coins possible.**

Name ______________________________

Compare Amounts to Prices

car	train	bike	plane	boat	bus

95¢	93¢	75¢	80¢	86¢	68¢

Write the amount. Write the names and prices of toys you could buy.

79¢

1 bus 68¢

2 ________ ________

____

3 ________ ________

4 ________ ________

____

5 ________ ________

6 ________ ________

Talk About It ■ **Reasoning**

Would you be able to buy the car if you have 89¢? Why or why not?

Practice

duck	giraffe	ladybug	tiger	lizard
65¢	70¢	90¢	79¢	85¢

Write the amount. Write the names and prices of toys you could buy.

75¢

1. giraffe 70¢
2. ________ ____

____

3. ________ ____
4. ________ ____

____

5. ________ ____
6. ________ ____

Algebra

7. You save 5¢ each day. You start on Monday. On Friday, how much have you saved? ________

Monday	Tuesday	Wednesday	Thursday	Friday

HOME ACTIVITY • **Ask your child to count out loud each group of coins.**

Name ______________________________

Make Change

Count on from the price to find the change.
Start with pennies and then use nickels or dimes.

1 You have 25¢. You buy

18¢, 19¢, 20¢, 25¢

Your change is 8¢.

2 You have 50¢. You buy

38¢, ______, ______, ______

Your change is ______.

3 You have 40¢. You buy

34¢, ______, ______

Your change is ______.

4 You have 30¢. You buy

22¢, ______, ______, ______, ______

Your change is ______.

Talk About It ■ **Reasoning**

How do you know if you have gotten the right amount of change?

Practice

Count on from the price to find the change.
Start with pennies first, then use nickels or dimes.

1 You have 50¢. You buy

38¢

39¢, 40¢, 50¢

Your change is 12¢.

2 You have 75¢. You buy

62¢

______, ______, ______, ______

Your change is ______.

3 You have 50¢. You buy

36¢

______, ______, ______, ______, ______

Your change is ______.

Problem Solving ■ Reasoning

Solve.

4 Hans buys a toy that costs 23¢. He gives the clerk some money and gets 2¢ change. How much money did Hans give the clerk?

The toy costs ______.

Hans gets ______ change.

Hans gave the clerk ______.

HOME ACTIVITY • When you buy items that cost less than 99¢, help your child count on from the price of the item to the amount given to the clerk to figure out the change you should get.

Name ______________________________

UNDERSTAND PLAN SOLVE CHECK

Problem Solving
Make a List

There are 5 coins in Ana's bag.
None of the coins is greater than 5¢.
What coins could there be?
Make a list to find out.

nickels	pennies	total amount
5	0	25¢

Talk About It ▪ Reasoning

If you know all the coins are nickels, how will your list change?

Practice

Check to make sure the total number of coins you use is always three.

There are 3 coins in Ana's bag. None of the coins is greater than 10¢. What coins could there be? Make a list to find out.

dimes	nickels	pennies	total amount
3	0	0	30¢

Math Journal

Write About It

Suppose you know that at least one of the coins is a penny. Explain how your list will change.

HOME ACTIVITY • Put three coins (none greater than 10¢) into a bag. Ask your child to make a list of the possible combinations of coins in the bag.

Name ______________________________

Review/Test
Chapter 8

CHECK ▪ Concepts and Skills

Use coins. Show the amount of money in two ways. Draw and label each coin.

1

Write the amount. Then show the same amount with the fewest coins. Draw and label each coin.

2

Count on from the price to find the change.

3 You have 30¢. You buy

23¢, ______, ______, ______

Your change is ______.

CHECK ▪ Problem Solving

Solve.

4 Ana has 2 coins in her bag. None of the coins is greater than 5¢. What coins could there be? Make a list to find out.

nickels	pennies	total amount

Standardized Test Prep
Chapters 1–8

Name ______________________________

Choose the best answer for questions 1–3.

1 What is the total amount?

27¢	67¢	47¢	90¢
○	○	○	○

2 Jacob bought a ball that cost 62¢. He paid 65¢. What should he say to count his change?

65	64, 65	63, 64, 65	65, 66, 67
○	○	○	○

3 What is the total amount of money?

Half-Dollar	Dimes	Nickels	Pennies	Total
1	1	2	3	?

73¢	72¢	70¢	48¢
○	○	○	○

Show What You Know

4 Write an amount that is less than $1.00. Draw coins to show the amount in two different ways.

CHAPTER 9 Telling Time

To	Track	Time
San Diego	2	2:00
Detroit	4	2:30
Boise	3	3:00
Orlando	1	8:45

How many minutes until the next train leaves? Ask other questions about time.

SCHOOL HOME CONNECTION

Dear Family,

Today we started Chapter 9. We will learn how to tell time. Here is the math vocabulary and an activity for us to do together at home.

Love,

____

My Math Words

minute
hour
digital clock

Vocabulary

minute A unit used to measure time. There are 60 minutes in one hour.

hour Another unit used to measure time. There are 60 minutes in one hour and 24 hours in one day.

digital clock A clock that shows digits for the hour and the minutes after the hour.
For example: 7:35 and 12:05

digital clock

Visit *The Learning Site* for additional ideas and activities. www.harcourtschool.com

ACTIVITY

Ask your child to tell you what time a favorite TV show starts and what time the show ends. Have him or her tell you how long the show lasts.

Books to Share

To read about telling time with your child, look for these books in your local library.

Clocks and More Clocks,
by Pat Hutchins,
Simon & Schuster,
1994.

The Boy Who Stopped Time,
by Anthony Taber,
Margaret K. McElderry Books, 1993.

Tuesday,
by David Wiesner,
Houghton Mifflin, 1997

Name ____________________

Tell Time to 5 Minutes

Write the time.

1

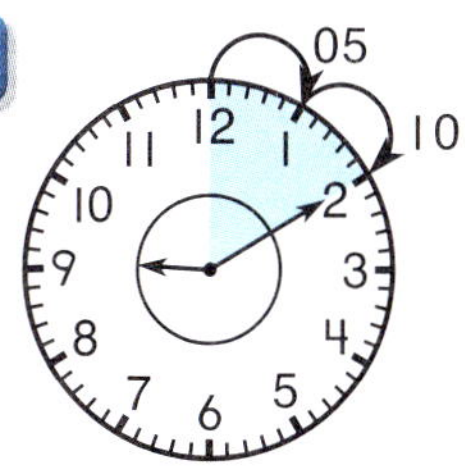

9:10

2

___ : ___

3

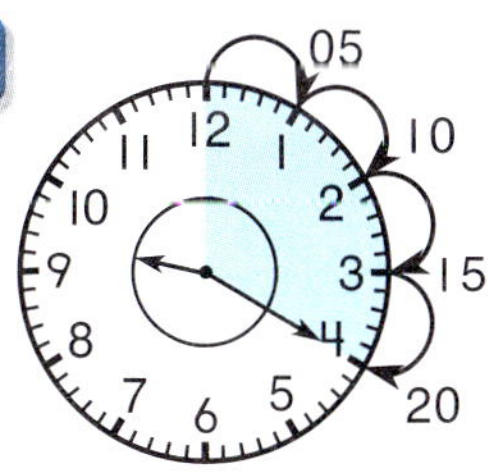

___ : ___

4

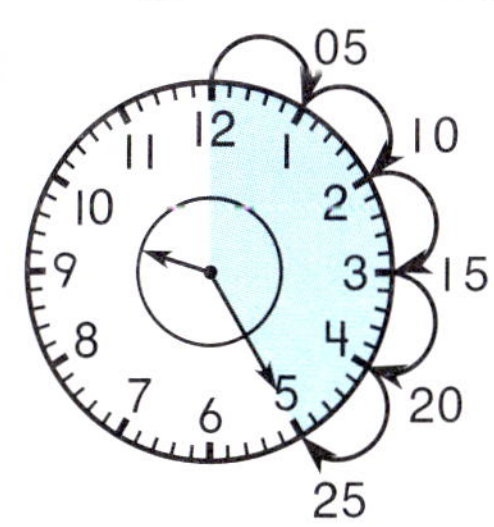

___ : ___

5

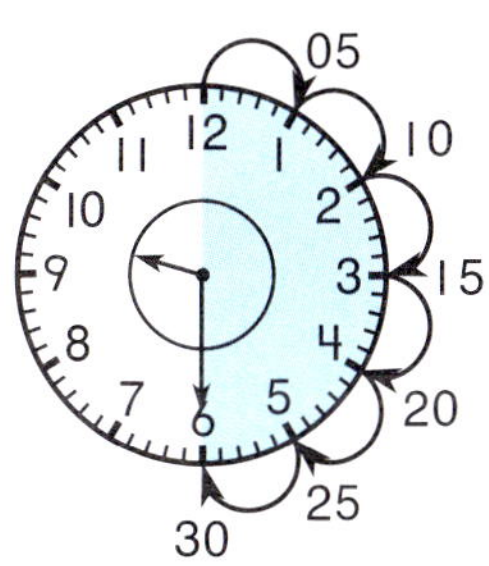

___ : ___

6

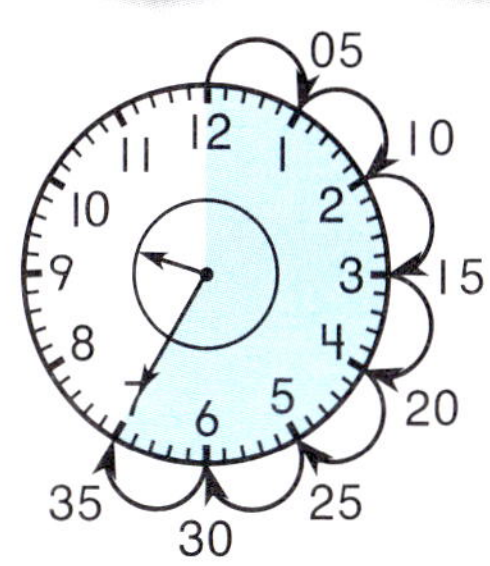

___ : ___

Talk About It ▪ **Reasoning**

When might it be important to know how to tell time to 5 minutes?

Practice

Write the time.

1 

5:15

2 

___:___

3 

___:___

4 

___:___

5 

___:___

6 

___:___

7 

___:___

8 

___:___

9 

___:___

Problem Solving ■ Visual Thinking

10 50 minutes after 2 o'clock is 2:50.
55 minutes after 2 o'clock is 2:55.
What time is 60 minutes after 2 o'clock?

___:___

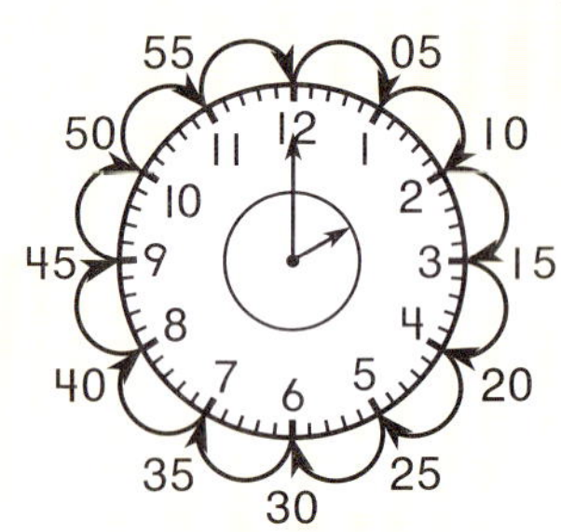

HOME ACTIVITY • At various times of the day, ask your child to tell you the time to 5 minutes.

Name ______________________________

Time After the Hour

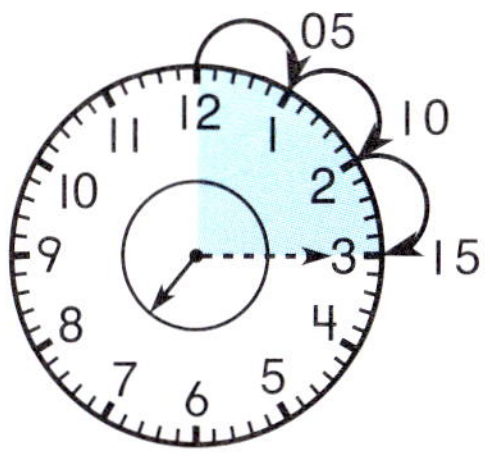

7:15

15 minutes after 7
quarter past 7

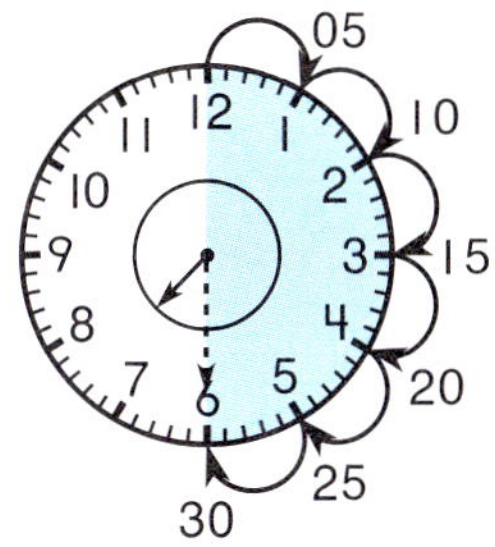

7:30

30 minutes after 7
half past 7

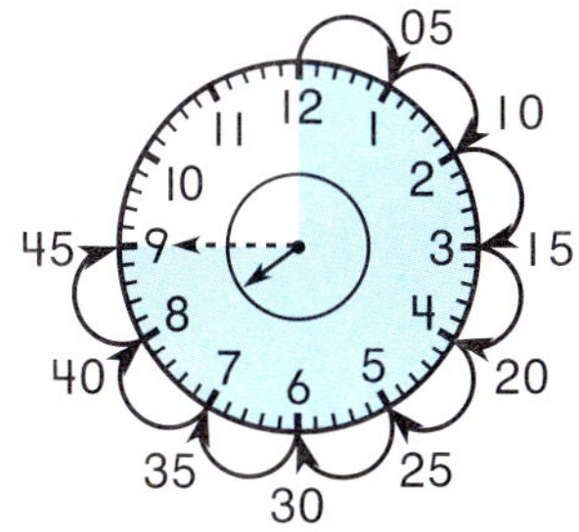

7:45

45 minutes after 7
quarter to 8

Draw the minute hand to show the time.
Write the time.

1 45 minutes after 10

10:45

2 quarter past 3

____ : ____

3 30 minutes after 4

____ : ____

4 45 minutes after 6

____ : ____

5 15 minutes after 11

____ : ____

6 half past 8

____ : ____

7 45 minutes after 2

____ : ____

8 half past 12

____ : ____

9 quarter past 5

____ : ____

Talk About It ■ Reasoning

Look at the clocks at the top of the page. How do they show why you could say that 7:30 is half past 7?

Practice

Draw the minute hand to show the time.
Write the time.

1 25 minutes after 6

6:25

2 10 minutes after 12

___ : ___

3 45 minutes after 3

___ : ___

4 quarter past 1

___ : ___

5 20 minutes after 6

___ : ___

6 half past 5

___ : ___

7 30 minutes after 4

___ : ___

8 5 minutes after 12

___ : ___

9 40 minutes after 10

___ : ___

Problem Solving ■ Application

Circle early or late.

10 Lunch is served at 12:30.
Juan gets there at 12:45.
Is Juan early or late?

early late

11 Sue is meeting Karen at 7:00.
Sue gets there at 6:45.
Is Sue early or late?

early late

HOME ACTIVITY • Use a clock at home. At the start of different activities, ask your child to tell the time to the nearest quarter hour and time after the hour.

Name ______________________

Time Before the Hour

Times after the half-hour are often given as before the next hour.

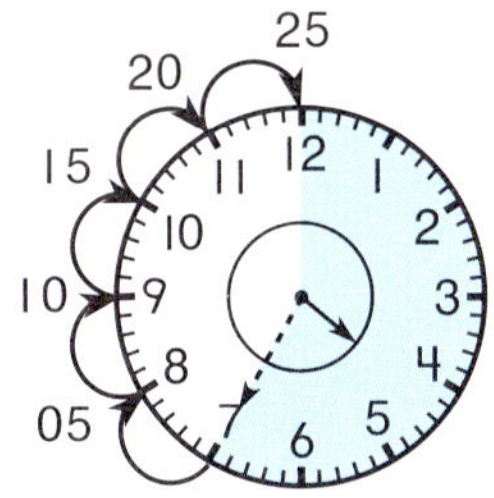

4:35
25 minutes before 5

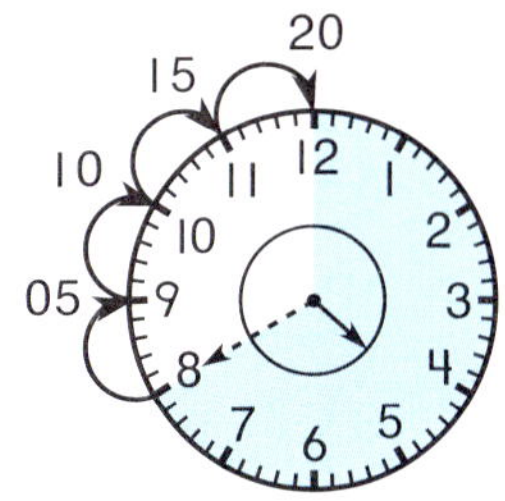

4:40
20 minutes before 5

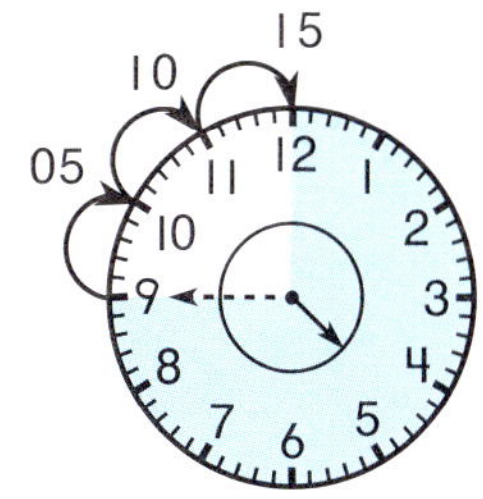

4:45
15 minutes before 5
quarter to 5

Draw the minute hand to show the time.
Write the time.

1 10 minutes before 5

4:50

2 quarter to 12

___ : ___

3 25 minutes before 4

___ : ___

4 quarter to 10

___ : ___

5 5 minutes before 6

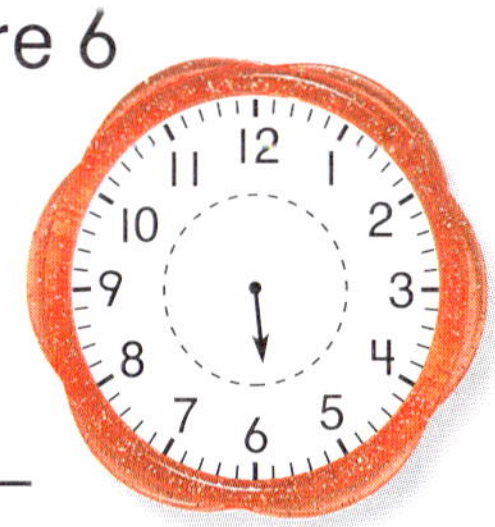

___ : ___

6 twenty minutes before 3

___ : ___

7 5 minutes before 7

___ : ___

8 15 minutes before 9

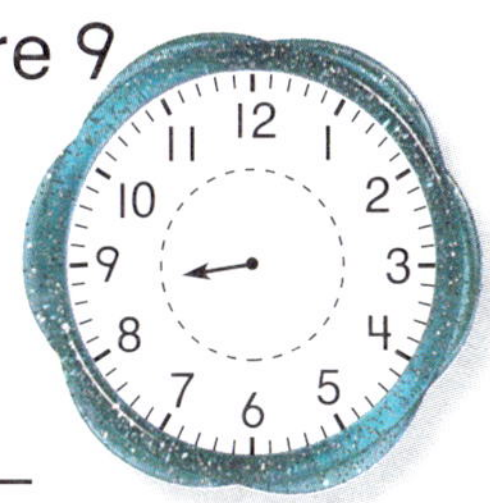

___ : ___

9 20 minutes before 5

___ : ___

Talk About It ■ Reasoning

How can 6:35 be before 7:00 and after 6:00?

Practice

Draw the minute hand to show the time.
Write the time.

1 5 minutes before 10

9:55

2 quarter to 11

___ : ___

3 20 minutes before 1

___ : ___

4 quarter to 6

___ : ___

5 10 minutes before 3

___ : ___

6 15 minutes before 6

___ : ___

7 25 minutes before 12

___ : ___

8 15 minutes before 9

___ : ___

9 quarter to 3

___ : ___

Algebra

10 Continue the pattern. Draw clock hands.

2:00 | 2:15 | 2:30 | 2:45 | 3:00

HOME ACTIVITY • At times from the half-hour to the hour during the day, ask your child to tell the time before the hour.

Name ______________________

UNDERSTAND PLAN SOLVE CHECK

Problem Solving
Use a Model

Draw the minute hand to show the time.
Write the time.

30 minutes later

4:15

4:45

1

10:00

15 minutes later

___ : ___

2

8:25

5 minutes later

___ : ___

3

3:40

25 minutes later

___ : ___

Practice

Draw the minute hand to show the time.
Write the time.

1

9:05

50 minutes later

9:55

2

11:35

35 minutes later

____ : ____

3

4:25

10 minutes later

____ : ____

Problem Solving ■ Estimating

Circle 1 second or 1 minute.

4 It takes about 1 second to sneeze. It takes about 1 minute to wash your hands. About how long does it take to tie your shoes?

1 second   1 minute

5 It takes about 1 second to blink your eyes. It takes about 1 minute to sharpen your pencil. About how long does it take to smile?

1 second   1 minute

HOME ACTIVITY • Have your child tell you the time every 5 minutes from 5 minutes to 55 minutes after the hour.

Name ______________________

Review/Test
Chapter 9

CHECK ■ Concepts and Skills

Write the time.

1 

___:___

2 

___:___

3 

___:___

Draw the minute hand to show the time. Write the time.

4 20 minutes after 6

___:___

5 half past 5

___:___

6 5 minutes after 10

___:___

7 10 minutes before 8

___:___

8 quarter to 1

___:___

9 20 minutes before 4

___:___

Draw the minute hand to show the time. Write the time.

10 

7:25

50 minutes later

___:___

Name ______________________________

Standardized Test Prep
Chapters 1–9

Choose the best answer for questions 1–4.

1 Shannece sees 12 kittens. Seven of them are black. The rest are white. How many are white?

4	5	19	20
○	○	○	○

2 What time does the clock show?

4:15	4:45
○	○
4:30	4:50
○	○

3 What time does the clock show?

quarter past 12	25 minutes after 12
○	○
20 minutes after 12	half past 12
○	○

4 What time does the clock show?

20 minutes before 10	30 minutes before 10
○	○
25 minutes before 10	quarter to 10
○	○

Show What You Know

5 Draw hands on the clock. Write the time.

Show a time that is 15 minutes past the hour.

___ : ___

Show the time that is 30 minutes later.

___ : ___

CHAPTER 10

Understanding Time

Write the month you think each picture shows.

SCHOOL HOME CONNECTION

Dear Family,

Today we started Chapter 10. We will use a calendar, learn about A.M. and P.M., and estimate time. Here is the math vocabulary and an activity for us to do together at home.

Love,

____

My Math Words

A.M.
P.M.
month
day
date
week

Vocabulary

A.M. is used to label the time between midnight and noon.

P.M. is used to label the time between noon and midnight.

month — January
day — Sunday
date — 5
week — 19 20 21 22 23 24 25

January						
Sunday	Monday	Tuesday	Wednesday	Thursday	Friday	Saturday
			1	2	3	4
5	6	7	8	9	10	11
12	13	14	15	16	17	18
19	20	21	22	23	24	25
26	27	28	29	30	31	

Visit *The Learning Site* for additional ideas and activities. www.harcourtschool.com

ACTIVITY

Help your child make a schedule of the activities that he or she does at home, such as homework, watching television, and helping with chores.

Books to Share

To read about time with your child, look for these books in your local library.

Benjamin's 365 Birthdays,
by Judi Barrett,
Aladdin, 1992.

Get Up & Go!,
by Stuart J. Murphy,
HarperCollins, 1996.

Morning, Noon, and Night,
by Jean Craighead George,
HarperCollins, 1999.

Name ______________________________

Daily Events

Time from **midnight** until **noon** is **A.M.** 9:00 A.M. is in the morning.

Time from noon until midnight is **P.M.** 9:00 P.M. is in the evening.

Write the correct time. Circle A.M. or P.M.

1 wake up

7:45 (A.M.) P.M.

2 eat lunch

____ : ____ A.M. P.M.

3 leave school

____ : ____ A.M. P.M.

4 go to bed

____ : ____ A.M. P.M.

Talk About It ■ Reasoning

Do children eat lunch at school at 11:30 A.M. or 11:30 P.M.? Explain your answer.

Practice

Write the correct time.
Circle A.M. or P.M.

1 have reading class

9:15 (A.M.) P.M.

2 do homework

____ : ____ A.M. P.M.

3 play soccer

____ : ____ A.M. P.M.

4 eat dinner

____ : ____ A.M. P.M.

5 get ready for bed

____ : ____ A.M. P.M.

6 sleep

____ : ____ A.M. P.M.

Mixed Review

7 Show 52¢ with the fewest coins.

HOME ACTIVITY • With your child, make a list of daily events and the time when you do each one. Be sure to use A.M. and P.M. when you write the times.

Name ______________________

UNDERSTAND PLAN SOLVE CHECK

Problem Solving
Use a Model

The hour hand moves from 11 to 1 to show 2 hours. The minute hand moves around the clock 2 times.

The party starts at 11:00 A.M.
It is over at 1:00 P.M.
How much time has passed?

UNDERSTAND

What do you want to find out?

PLAN

You can use a model to solve the problem.

SOLVE

2 hours

CHECK

Does your answer make sense? Explain.

Use a clock to help solve the problem.
Write how much time has passed.

1. Jack starts playing the piano at 2:00 P.M. He plays until 2:20 P.M. How much time has passed?

   20 minutes

2. School starts at 9:00 A.M. It ends at 3:00 P.M. How much time has passed?

   ______ hours

3. Peter starts playing kickball at 3:30 P.M. He plays until 5:30 P.M. How much time has passed?

   ______ hours

4. Judy starts her homework at 6:30 P.M. She finishes at 7:00 P.M. How much time has passed?

   ______ minutes

Practice

Use a clock to help solve the problem.
Write how much time has passed.

1. Rabbit got to the bus stop at 2:00 P.M. It is now 4:00 P.M. How much time has passed?

   2 hours

2. Rabbit's aunt puts the cake in the oven at 2:15 P.M. She takes it out at 2:45 P.M. How much time has passed?

   _______ minutes

3. Rabbit practices violin from 8:45 P.M. until 9:15 P.M. How much time has passed?

   _______ minutes

4. The soccer tournament starts at 11:00 A.M. It is over at 4:00 P.M. How much time has passed?

   _______ hours

5. Breakfast starts at 7:30 A.M. It is over at 7:45 A.M. How much time has passed?

   _______ minutes

6. Rabbit sleeps from 9:00 P.M. until 7:00 A.M. How much time has passed?

   _______ hours

7. Rabbit watches TV from 6:30 P.M. to 9:30 P.M. How much time has passed?

   _______ hours

8. The plane takes off at 2:00 P.M. It lands at 3:00 P.M. How much time has passed?

   _______ hour

Math Journal

Write About It

Write a story problem like those on this page. Give the starting time and the ending time for an activity. Ask a classmate to solve your problem.

HOME ACTIVITY • With your child, write down the starting and ending times for an activity you do. Find out how much time passes while you do it. Repeat several times during the day.

Name ______________________

Use a Calendar

Use the **calendar** to answer the questions.

There are 7 days in 1 week.

NOVEMBER

Sunday	Monday	Tuesday	Wednesday	Thursday	Friday	Saturday
					1	2
3	4	5	6	7	8	9
10	11	12	13	14	15	16
17	18	19	20	21	22	23
24	25	26	27	28 Thanksgiving	29	30

1. What is the date of the third Tuesday? November 19

2. How many days are in this month? ______

3. What is the day and date one week before Thanksgiving? ______, ______

4. What is the date one week after November 7? ______

5. On which day will the next month start? ______

Talk About It ■ Reasoning

How does a calendar help you keep track of your activities?

Practice

There are 52 **weeks** in 1 year.
There are 12 **months** in 1 **year**.

Use the calendar to answer the questions.

January

Su	M	T	W	Th	F	Sa
			1	2	3	4
5	6	7	8	9	10	11
12	13	14	15	16	17	18
19	20	21	22	23	24	25
26	27	28	29	30	31	

February

Su	M	T	W	Th	F	Sa
						1
2	3	4	5	6	7	8
9	10	11	12	13	14	15
16	17	18	19	20	21	22
23	24	25	26	27	28	

March

Su	M	T	W	Th	F	Sa
						1
2	3	4	5	6	7	8
9	10	11	12	13	14	15
16	17	18	19	20	21	22
23	24	25	26	27	28	29
30	31					

April

Su	M	T	W	Th	F	Sa
		1	2	3	4	5
6	7	8	9	10	11	12
13	14	15	16	17	18	19
20	21	22	23	24	25	26
27	28	29	30			

May

Su	M	T	W	Th	F	Sa
				1	2	3
4	5	6	7	8	9	10
11	12	13	14	15	16	17
18	19	20	21	22	23	24
25	26	27	28	29	30	31

June

Su	M	T	W	Th	F	Sa
1	2	3	4	5	6	7
8	9	10	11	12	13	14
15	16	17	18	19	20	21
22	23	24	25	26	27	28
29	30					

July

Su	M	T	W	Th	F	Sa
		1	2	3	4	5
6	7	8	9	10	11	12
13	14	15	16	17	18	19
20	21	22	23	24	25	26
27	28	29	30	31		

August

Su	M	T	W	Th	F	Sa
					1	2
3	4	5	6	7	8	9
10	11	12	13	14	15	16
17	18	19	20	21	22	23
24	25	26	27	28	29	30
31						

September

Su	M	T	W	Th	F	Sa
	1	2	3	4	5	6
7	8	9	10	11	12	13
14	15	16	17	18	19	20
21	22	23	24	25	26	27
28	29	30				

October

Su	M	T	W	Th	F	Sa
			1	2	3	4
5	6	7	8	9	10	11
12	13	14	15	16	17	18
19	20	21	22	23	24	25
26	27	28	29	30	31	

November

Su	M	T	W	Th	F	Sa
						1
2	3	4	5	6	7	8
9	10	11	12	13	14	15
16	17	18	19	20	21	22
23	24	25	26	27	28	29
30						

December

Su	M	T	W	Th	F	Sa
	1	2	3	4	5	6
7	8	9	10	11	12	13
14	15	16	17	18	19	20
21	22	23	24	25	26	27
28	29	30	31			

1. With which month does the year begin?  January

2. Which month follows October?  ____________

3. Which month has the fewest days?  ____________

4. Which is the fifth month in the year?  ____________

5. What is the date one week after May 28?  ____________

HOME ACTIVITY • Point out a date on a calendar. Ask your child to tell you the days and dates one week before and one week after that date.

Name ______________________________

Estimate Time

About how long will it take?

to eat lunch

about 15 minutes

about 15 hours

to play a soccer game

about 1 month

about 1 hour

About how long will it take?
Circle the reasonable estimate.

1. to take a trip

5 minutes   5 days

2. to paint a house

3 days   3 minutes

3. to brush your teeth

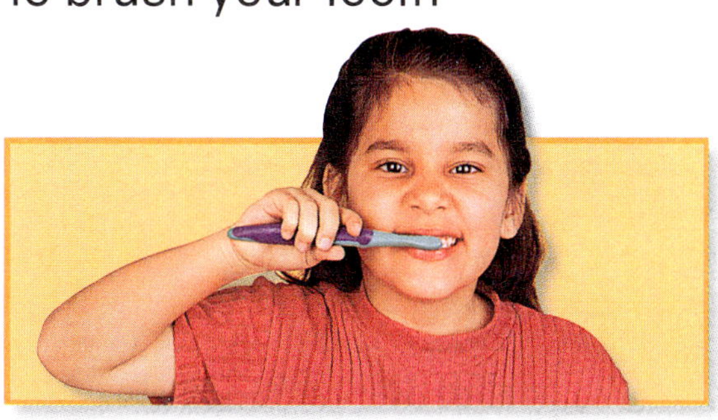

4 minutes   4 hours

4. to complete second grade

10 months   10 days

Talk About It ■ **Reasoning**

What activities take hours to do?
What activities take minutes to do?

Practice

About how long will it take?
Circle the reasonable estimate.

1 to build a house

8 days — (8 months)

2 to walk the dog

10 minutes — 10 hours

3 to eat dinner

30 minutes — 30 days

4 to watch a game

2 weeks — 2 hours

5 to count to 100

1 minute — 1 week

6 to wash the car

1 month — 1 hour

HOME ACTIVITY • Ask your child to estimate whether it would take minutes, hours, days, weeks, or months to sail around the world, watch a movie, and brush his or her teeth.

Name ______________________________

Time Relationships

Algebra

We tell time in minutes, hours, days, weeks, months, and years.

Time Relationships	
There are 60 minutes in 1 hour.	There are 24 hours in 1 day.
There are 7 days in 1 week.	There are 28, 30, or 31 days in 1 month.
There are 12 months in 1 year.	There are 52 weeks in 1 year.

Write more than, less than, or the same as for each sentence.

1. Mira went to live with her grandparents for one year. This is

   the same as 52 weeks.

2. She was on the plane for 3 hours. This is

   ____________________ 1 day.

3. Mira had some good friends after 7 days. This is

   ____________________ 1 month.

4. Mira went home after 12 months. This is

   ____________________ 1 year.

Talk About It ■ **Reasoning**

Explain your answers to the questions on this page.

Practice

Write more than, less than, or the same as for each sentence.

Time Relationships
There are 60 minutes in 1 hour.
There are 24 hours in 1 day.
There are 7 days in 1 week.
There are 28, 30, or 31 days in 1 month.
There are 12 months in 1 year.
There are 52 weeks in 1 year.

1. Every fall, Paulo plays soccer for 3 months. This is

less than 52 weeks.

2. Before practice, Paulo warms up for 15 minutes. This is

________________ 1 hour.

3. The games last for about 2 hours. This is

________________ 60 minutes.

Problem Solving ■ Visual Thinking

Estimate and write the time.

4. Tara started painting the fence at 8:00. It is 11:00 now. What time do you think she will finish? ___:___

© Harcourt

HOME ACTIVITY • Suggest different activities and ask your child how long he or she estimates each would take.

Name ______________________________

Review/Test
Chapter 10

CHECK ■ Concepts and Skills

Write the correct time.
Circle A.M. or P.M.

1 make dinner

___:___ A.M. P.M.

About how long will it take?
Circle the reasonable estimate.

2 to wash your hands

1 minute 1 hour

Use a calendar to answer the question.

3 What is the date of the second Friday in November?

____

Write more than, less than, or the same as.

4 Mark's baby sister is 6 weeks old.

This is ______________ 1 month.

CHECK ■ Problem Solving

Use a (clock) to help solve the problem.
Write how much time has passed.

5 Annie starts playing a game at 4:15 P.M. She stops at 4:45 P.M. How much time has passed?

______ minutes

Name ______________________________

Standardized Test Prep
Chapters 1–10

Choose the best answer for questions 1–4.

1 Which would you do at 9:00 P.M.?

go to school	go to bed	eat dinner	plant flowers
○	○	○	○

2 Matthew slept from 10:00 P.M. until 8:00 A.M.
How much time passed?

8 minutes	8 hours	10 minutes	10 hours
○	○	○	○

3 Which is more than 1 hour?

16 minutes	72 minutes	60 minutes	26 minutes
○	○	○	○

4 What is the value of the underlined digit?

8<u>6</u>

6	60	8	80
○	○	○	○

Show What You Know

5 Use a clock. Complete the chart.
Choose your own times. Make Sara's baseball game last longer than John's soccer game.

Games	Starting Time	Ending Time	How Long?
Sara's baseball game			
John's soccer game			

Grandma Rabbit's Birthday

written by Lucy Floyd
illustrated byTerri Chicko

This book will help me review time and money.

This book belongs to ____________________.

A

Rabbit was very excited. Today was Grandma Rabbit's birthday! "Grandma's birthday party is at 3:00," said Rabbit. "I must buy a gift for her! Let me see.

I have $____.____."

On the way to the store, Rabbit met Toad. "Where are you going in such a hurry, Rabbit?" asked Toad.

"Today is Grandma Rabbit's birthday, and I must buy a gift for her!" said Rabbit.

"The party is at 3:00! My watch says ___:___."

Rabbit showed Toad his coins. "You have too many coins," Toad said. "You could lose some. Let me help you. You have $1.00. I can make the same amount with fewer coins. Trade with me."

Circle the coins that Toad can trade with Rabbit.

D

Rabbit went on his way and soon met Squirrel. "Where are you going in such a hurry, Rabbit?" asked Squirrel.

"Today is Grandma Rabbit's birthday, and I must buy a gift for her," said Rabbit.

"The party is at 3:00! My watch says ___:___."

Rabbit showed Squirrel his coins. “You have too many coins,” Squirrel said. “You could lose some. Let me help you. You have $1.00. I can make the same amount with fewer coins. Trade with me.”

Circle the coins that Squirrel can trade with Rabbit.

Rabbit went on his way and soon met Chipmunk. “Where are you going in such a hurry, Rabbit?” asked Chipmunk.

“Today is Grandma Rabbit’s birthday, and I must buy a gift for her,” said Rabbit.

“The party is at 3:00! My watch says ___:___.”

Rabbit showed Chipmunk his coins. "You have too many coins," Chipmunk said. "You could lose some. Let me help you. You have $1.00. I can make the same amount with fewer coins. Trade with me."

Circle the coins that Chipmunk can trade with Rabbit.

Rabbit looked at all the things in the store. "I want to buy the very best gift for Grandma Rabbit," he said.

"My watch says __:__."

How many minutes does Rabbit have to get to the party?_____ minutes

"Hurray!" said Rabbit. "I got to the birthday party on time, and I have a gift for Grandma!"

Name ___________________________

Problem Solving
Math Detective

Discover the Date

Use your reasoning skills and the calendar clues to solve each case.

May						
Sunday	Monday	Tuesday	Wednesday	Thursday	Friday	Saturday
		1	2	3	4	5
6	7	8	9	10	11	12
13	14	15	16	17	18	19
20	21	22	23	24	25	26
27	28	29	30	31		

Clue 1:
The date is a double.

Clue 2:
It is **not** an odd number.

Clue 3:
It is in the third week of May.

Clue 4:
It is the fourth day of the week.

What is the date? ________

Clue 1:
The date is **not** an even number.

Clue 2:
The digit in the tens place is even.

Clue 3:
It is not Sunday.

Clue 4:
It is in the last week of May.
What is the date? ________

Stretch Your Thinking Choose a date in May and make up clues that will help a classmate discover it.

Name ______________________________

Challenge
Coin Toss

If you toss a penny, is it more likely to land heads up or tails up?

Try it. You will need 1 penny. Toss a penny 10 times.
For each toss, make a tally mark to show heads or tails.

Sides	Tally Marks	Totals
heads		
tails		

1. How many times did the coin land heads up? ______

2. How many times did the coin land tails up? ______

3. Did the coin land heads up or tails up more often? ______

If you toss the penny 20 times, will it land more often on one side than the other? Write your prediction.

____

____

Name ______________________

Study Guide and Review

Skills and Concepts

Write the total amount.

1  ______

2  ______

Use coins. Draw and label each coin.

3 Show the same amount using the fewest coins.

4 David bought a ball that costs 32¢. He paid 35¢. Count on from the price to find the change.

33¢, ______ , ______

Your change is ______.

5 Write the time.

______

6 Write the time before the hour.

______

Write the correct time and circle A.M. or P.M.

7

___:___ A.M. P.M.

8

___:___ A.M. P.M.

Use the calendar to answer the questions.

9 What is the date one week after May 3? _______

10 How many days are in this month? _______

Circle the correct answer.

11 About how long will it take to eat breakfast?

15 minutes 15 days

12 Chris's puppy is 7 days old.

This is ________________ 1 week.

more than less than

the same as

Problem Solving

13 Karen wants to buy a pen. Draw the coins she will need.

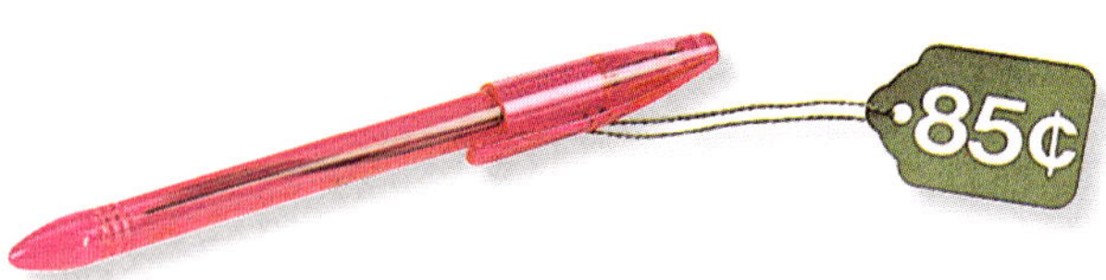

Name ______________________________

Stuck on You

Jane wants to buy these 2 stickers.

- She has 55¢ in her pocket.
- She has more than 3 coins, but less than 10 coins.

Show 2 ways Jane can have the coins in her pocket. How much money will Jane have left after she buys the stickers?

Show your work.

Technology

Name ______________________________

Mighty Math Zoo Zillions • Count Money

1. Click .
2. Click .
3. Click E.
4. Play 5 times.

Practice and Problem Solving

Use coins. Draw and label the coins to show the amount.

1. 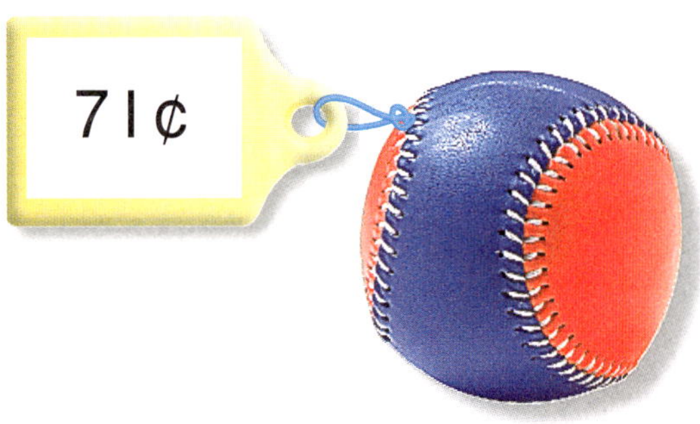

2. Use coins. Draw 2 ways to make 53¢.

Name ______________________________

PROBLEM SOLVING ON LOCATION

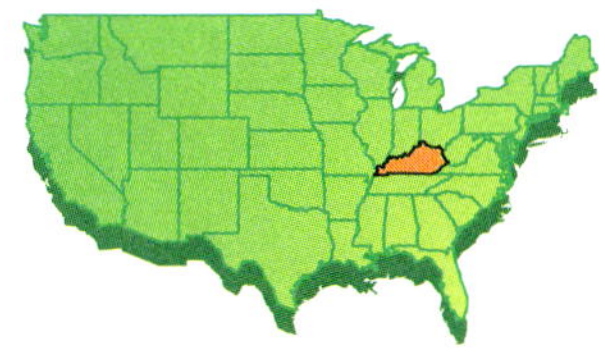

In the Caves

Mammoth Cave, in Kentucky, is the longest group of connected caves in the world.

Tours and Times	
Historic Tour (1 hour long)	9:00, 10:00, 1:00
Frozen Niagara Tour (2 hours long)	9:00, 1:00
Violet City Tour (2 hours long)	10:00, 2:00
Wild Cave Tour (1 hour long)	9:00, 11:00, 3:00

Plan a day at Mammoth Cave. Go on each tour. Complete the chart.

Tour	Start Time	End Time
Lunch	12:00	1:00

Name ______________________

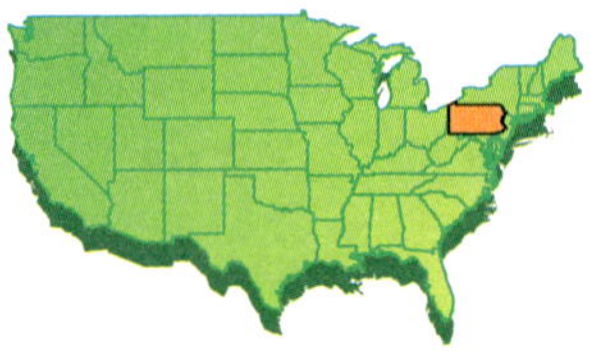

PROBLEM SOLVING ON LOCATION

At the Mint

Coins are made at the United States mints. The first mint in our country was in Philadelphia, Pennsylvania.

A coin press makes a different coin each day. It makes 4 coins every minute. Find out which coin it makes on each day.

penny

quarter

nickel

dime

Use coins. Draw to show your work.
Write the name of the coin.

On Monday, it makes 4¢ every minute. ______________	On Tuesday, it makes 20¢ every minute. ______________
On Wednesday, it makes 40¢ every minute. ______________	On Thursday, it makes $1.00 every minute. ______________